Why Do the Lights Turn On?

by Barbara J. Davis

Science and Curriculum Consultant: Debra Voege, M.A.,
Science Curriculum Resource Teacher

An Imprint of Chelsea House Publishers

Science in the Real World: Why Do the Lights Turn On?

Copyright © 2010 by Infobase Publishing

All rights reserved. No part of this book may be reproduced or utilized in any form or by any means, electronic or mechanical, including photocopying, recording, or by any information storage or retrieval systems, without permission in writing from the publisher. For information contact:

Chelsea Clubhouse
An imprint of Chelsea House Publishers
132 West 31st Street
New York NY 10001

Library of Congress Cataloging-in-Publication Data
Davis, Barbara J., 1952-
    Why do the lights turn on? / Barbara J. Davis; science and curriculum consultant, Debra Voege.
       p. cm. — (Science in the real world)
    Includes index.
    ISBN 978-1-60413-471-1
    1. Electricity—Juvenile literature. I. Title. II. Series.
  QC527.2.D39 2010
  537—dc22
                                      2009013432

Chelsea Clubhouse books are available at special discounts when purchased in bulk quantities for businesses, associations, institutions, or sales promotions. Please call our Special Sales Department in New York at (212) 967-8800 or (800) 322-8755.

You can find Chelsea Clubhouse on the World Wide Web at http://www.chelseahouse.com

Developed for Chelsea House by RJF Publishing LLC (www.RJFpublishing.com)
Text and cover design by Tammy West/Westgraphix LLC
Illustrations by Spectrum Creative Inc.
Photo research by Edward A. Thomas
Index by Nila Glikin

Photo Credits: 4: Pixmann Limited/Photolibrary; 5, 9, 10, 22, 25: iStockphoto; 7: © Christopher Morris/Corbis; 15: Andersen Ross/Photolibrary (boy at refrigerator), Guy Cali/Photolibrary (girl at laptop); 16: Tanya Constantine/Photolibrary; 18: Lester Lefkowitz/Photolibrary; 19: Getty Images; 22, 24, 29: © Edward A. Thomas; 28: Chris Ryan/Photolibrary.

Printed and bound in the United States of America

Bang RJF 10 9 8 7 6 5 4 3 2 1

This book is printed on acid-free paper.

All links and Web addresses were checked and verified to be correct at the time of publication. Because of the dynamic nature of the Web, some addresses and links may have changed since publication and may no longer be valid.

Table of Contents

An Electrical World 4
What Is Electricity? 6
Static Electricity 8
Electric Current 10
Circuits and Switches 12
Measuring Current 14
Volts and Watts 16
Making Electricity 18
Spinning Turbines 20
Moving Electricity 22
In the Home 24
Sharing Electricity 26
Looking to the Future 28
Glossary 30
To Learn More 31
Index 32

Words that are defined in the Glossary are in **bold** type the first time they appear in the text.

An Electrical World

What do you know about electricity? It's a huge part of modern daily life. It's so common, in fact, that most of us don't think about it all. Try listing ten things that you use every day that run on electricity. Many people would list things like televisions, DVD players, house lights, and computers. There are other things, though, that you might not think of right away. The refrigerator that keeps your food cold runs on electricity. So does the microwave that sometimes heats up your food. So does the dishwasher that cleans the dishes after a meal.

TVs, DVD players, and all kinds of devices around the home run on electricity.

In many factories, electricity runs all kinds of machines. These machines might put your favorite soft drink in a can. Machines lift heavy objects and move them from place to place. Automobile parts are cut and assembled by machines that use electricity. Even your favorite amusement park ride depends on electricity to run.

Electricity lights up the streets and buildings of New York City, as seen here from the top of a skyscraper.

Why Electricity Is So Useful

Electricity is really useful because it can easily be changed into heat, movement, and light. It can be made in one place and then sent over wires for long distances to where it is needed. Without electricity, life would be very different. Just think about what you would do if you had to go a week without using any of the things on your list.

DID YOU KNOW?

The White Way

As useful as electricity is, it's been put to widespread use only over the past 100 years or so. In 1879, Cleveland, Ohio, became the first U.S. city to use electric street lights. During the early 1900s, most large American cities started using them on their main roads. During this time, the term "white way" was used to describe a street with lights.

What Is Electricity?

Electricity is a form of energy. It is the movement of charged particles in **matter**. All matter is made up of tiny particles that are called **atoms**.

Atoms are made up of even smaller particles called **protons**, **neutrons**, and **electrons**. Protons carry a positive charge. Neutrons have no charge. Electrons carry a negative charge. The protons and neutrons are found in the nucleus, or center, of the atom. The electrons zip around the nucleus.

An atom usually has the same number of protons and electrons.

An atom is made up of protons and neutrons, which are in its nucleus, and electrons, which circle around the nucleus.

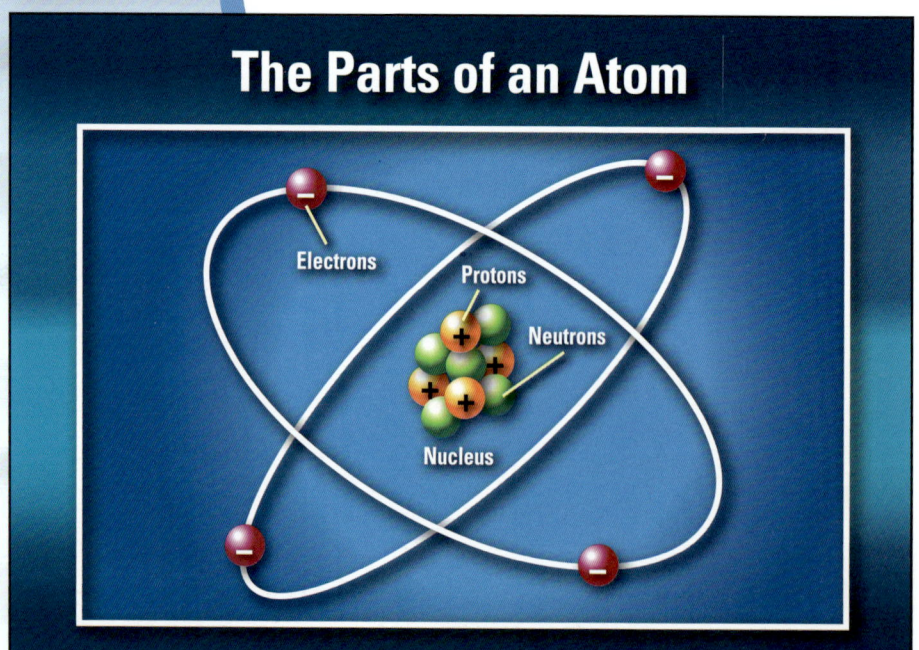

So it has the same number of positive charges from the protons as it has negative charges from the electrons. This means that the atom itself does not have a charge. It is what is called neutral. An atom can gain or lose electrons, though. If an atom gains electrons, it becomes negatively charged. If it loses electrons, it becomes positively charged.

Attracted and Repelled

When charged particles are close enough, they affect each other. Particles of the same charge push each other away. They are said to **repel** each other. Two positively charged particles will repel each other. So will two negatively charged particles. Particles with opposite charges, though, are drawn to each other. A negatively charged particle is said to be **attracted** to a positively charged particle. All of this movement of particles toward or away is the source of electricity.

DID YOU KNOW?

Benjamin Franklin and Electricity

Benjamin Franklin, who lived from 1706 to 1790, was an American statesman and one of the Founding Fathers of the United States. He was also a great scientist. In the 1700s, he did many experiments to try to understand electricity. Franklin was one of the first people to propose the theory that objects can have positive or negative charges and that objects attract or repel each other based on those charges.

Static Electricity

Have you ever noticed that things like sweaters and socks taken out of a clothes dryer sometimes stick together? That is a common example of static electricity. "Static" means "at rest." Static electricity is caused when there is a build-up of an electrical charge in one place.

Electrons can be knocked off atoms pretty easily. Rubbing two objects together causes electrons to move from one surface to another. When clothes are being tumbled in a dryer, they are knocking against each other. The different items of clothing develop an electric charge. Some pieces of clothing will lose electrons and have a positive charge. Other pieces will pick up electrons and have a negative charge. Opposite charges attract each other. This is why socks can end up stuck to a sweater!

Static electricity that builds up on an object sometimes may "jump" to another object that is close to it. This type of jump is called an electrical discharge.

Electric Shocks

Most of us have experienced what happens when we walk across a carpet and then touch a metal doorknob. That electric shock at the fingertips always comes as a surprise. Have you ever wondered why this happens? When you walk across a carpet, your shoes rub electrons off the carpet. The electrons build up in your body. When you touch the metal doorknob, the electrons move through you to the doorknob. You may even see a small spark and hear a crackling noise.

DID YOU KNOW?

Electricity in the Sky

The build-up and discharge of static electricity is a normal part of nature. Those black storm clouds that you sometimes see in the sky are a good example. Storm clouds have drops of water in them that are moving toward the ground. The clouds also have bits of ice in them. The moving drops of water and bits of ice rub against each other. Static electricity builds up. A negative charge forms at the bottom of the cloud. When the static electricity discharges from the cloud, the sky becomes bright with lightning, as in the photo above.

Electric Current

In an electrical discharge, electrons move very quickly for a short time and then stop. An electric **current** is a stream of electrons moving continuously along a path from one place to another. Electric currents bring electricity to many of the things we use today: the TV, the microwave, the lights that may be helping you to read this book.

Electric currents travel along **conductors**. These are materials through which electrons easily move. Copper is one of the best conductors of electric currents. This is why wires meant to carry electricity are often made of copper.

Because the filament in a light bulb does not conduct electricity well, it gets hot and glows, which makes a light bulb bright.

Why Light Bulbs Are Bright

For example, copper is commonly used in lamp cords. Electrons move along the copper wire and up to the light bulb. The light bulb also has a conductor. It is the thin wire inside the bulb called the **filament**. The filament is made of a metal such as tungsten. This metal is not as good a conductor as copper. Therefore, the electrons cannot move as easily along tungsten. When the electrons are slowed down, some of their electrical energy is changed to heat. The filament gets hot, and as it does, it glows. This is what produces the light in the light bulb.

The copper wire of a lamp cord is covered in a rubber-like material. This material is an **insulator**. Electrons cannot move easily through insulators. So the insulator on the outside of the lamp cord keeps the electrons traveling along the wire. You can touch the outside of the cord and not get an electric shock. Rubber and some types of plastic are examples of insulators.

DID YOU KNOW?

A Human Conductor

The human body is 90 percent water. Water is an excellent conductor of electricity. This means electricity can pass through the human body quite easily.

Circuits and Switches

Electric current often travels in a path called an electric **circuit**. An electric circuit is a closed loop. This means that the electricity follows the same path through the circuit over and over again. Today, just about all buildings have electric circuits inside their walls. This includes homes, schools, stores, theaters, factories, and other businesses. The lights on the ceiling are connected to electric circuits. Anything that is plugged into a wall outlet is being connected to an electric circuit. This includes lamps, TVs, computers, refrigerators, and many other things. But why don't the lights and all of these other

Flipping a switch either closes or breaks a circuit, which can make a bulb light or go off.

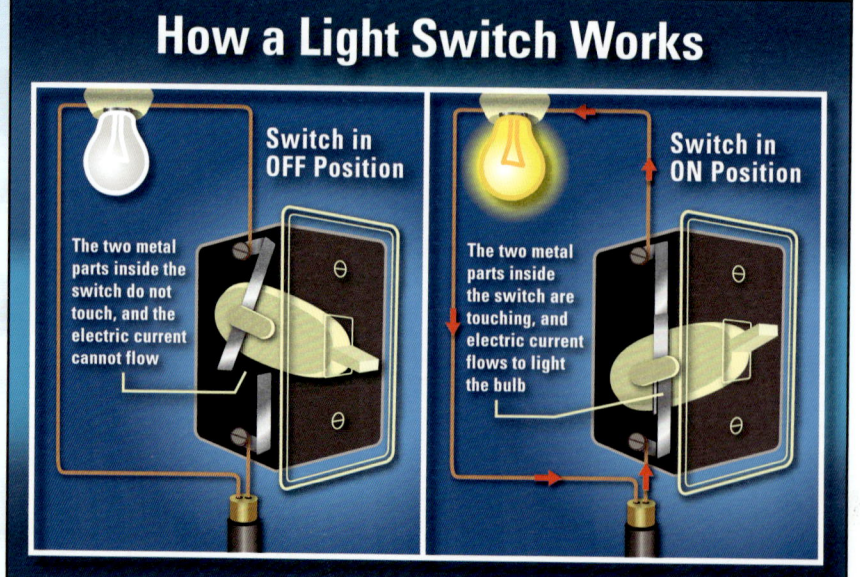

things stay on all the time if they're connected to circuits?

How Switches Work

The answer is: **switches**. Usually a wall switch connected to a circuit can turn a ceiling light on or off. Lamps have on/off switches, and so do almost all electrical devices. But how do switches work?

Remember that an electric circuit has to be a closed loop for electricity to flow through it. A switch can either break that loop or keep it closed. Inside the switch are two metal parts that conduct electricity. When a light switch on the wall or the switch on a lamp is flipped to the ON position, the two metal parts touch each other. The circuit is closed, and electricity flows through the switch to light the bulb. When a switch is flipped to the OFF position, the metal parts are separated. The circuit is broken. Electricity cannot flow to the bulb. The light goes off.

DID YOU KNOW?

How Does a Flashlight Work?

Most flashlights get their electricity from one or more batteries inside. A circuit connects the battery to the flashlight's bulb. When you turn on the flashlight, you are flipping a switch to the ON position. This closes the circuit and lights the bulb. When you turn off the flashlight, you are flipping a switch to the OFF position and breaking the circuit. The bulb goes out.

Measuring Current

Circuits can carry different amounts of electricity. Special units are used to measure electricity. To understand these units, first imagine sitting by a river with many sticks floating in it. If the river current is slow, a few sticks may float by each second. If the river current is very fast, a lot of sticks will pass in front of you each second. Electric currents can be thought of in a similar way. Instead of sticks in water, though, the current is the flow of electrons.

The flow is measured at a point in the circuit. The measurement is of the number of electrons flowing past that point per second. This flow is measured in units called **amperes**, or amps for short. The symbol for amperes is A. One ampere is about 6 quintillion electrons. That is 6 billion billion electrons!

How Many Amps?

A simple circuit in a flashlight powered by a battery might have a current of 1 or 2 amps. Machines and other things that run on electricity

need a certain amount of current to operate. An average computer uses about 2 amps. Large appliances like refrigerators use much more than that—about 10 amps. Some electrical devices such as large motors might use as many as 20 amps.

Many home computers use about 2 amps of electricity. Refrigerators use as much as 10 amps.

DID YOU KNOW ?

One-Way and Two-Way Current

There are two types of electric currents that flow through circuits. In one type, the electrons always flow in the same direction. This is called **direct current** or DC. Batteries are sources of DC. In another type, the electrons are changing direction very often and moving back and forth through the circuit. This is called **alternating current** or AC. The electricity that comes into your town or city is AC.

Volts and Watts

Hair dryers in the United States are made to run on 110 volts of electricity.

Electric currents need a push to make them flow. The amount of push is called **voltage**. It is measured in units called **volts** (abbreviated V). The higher the voltage, the greater the push. Batteries and other devices have voltage ratings. Perhaps you've noticed something like "9V" on a battery. That means the battery can supply 9 volts of push.

Devices that run on electricity need a specific voltage to work properly. In the United States, most electrical devices around the home run on 110 volts. This voltage provides enough current flow for these devices. Some machines, such as a clothes washer, might need 220 volts. This level of voltage delivers more current to the machine.

What Is a Watt?

Flowing current gives off energy that can be used to do such things as make a bulb light, make a fan spin, or make a hair dryer get hot. The amount of energy given up every second by a current is called power. Power is measured in units called **watts**. One watt of power is equal to one volt pushing one amp through a wire.

You have probably noticed watt ratings on appliances or light bulbs. The ratings show the greatest number of watts the device will use. A 100 W (watt) light bulb will use no more than 100 watts of electric power while it is on.

A computer that is rated at 300 watts will use that much power only when all of its drives are working hard. Often, a computer will use only 65 watts of power or less at any given time.

DID YOU KNOW?

Voltage in Other Countries

Most appliances made to be used in North America and Japan need 110-volt current to operate. In most other parts of the world, though, the electric current in homes and other buildings is 220-volt current. That is why Americans traveling to different parts of the world often need special converters in order to run things like hair dryers or electric shavers they may bring with them. Converters change the voltage from 220 to 110.

Making Electricity

In 1831, an English scientist named Michael Faraday made a discovery. He found that moving a loop of wire around a magnet produced an electric current in the wire. Moving a magnet around a wire also produced electric current. This led Faraday to make the first **generator**. A generator is a machine that changes mechanical energy (energy from motion) into electrical energy. Generators use magnets and metal wire to produce electricity.

Magnets are surrounded by a force called a magnetic field. You can see this field in action if you slide a paper clip toward a magnet. When the paper clip gets close enough, the

The worker in this power plant standing on top of a generator looks tiny in relation to the huge size of the machine.

magnetic field pulls the paper clip onto the magnet. The magnet in a generator also has a magnetic field. A loop or coil of wire moves in the magnetic field. Sometimes it is the magnet that spins within a coil. In either case, electrons are forced by the magnetic field to flow through the wire. Electricity is created by the movement of these electrons.

Power Plant Generators

The electricity that comes into a town or city—and all the buildings within that area—is made at an electric power plant. A power plant generator uses huge magnets and metal coils. Some are as large as a house. A spinning coil in a power plant generator can produce as much as 25,000 volts of electricity.

DID YOU KNOW?

Michael Faraday
Michael Faraday (see photo above) was one of the most important scientists of the 1800s. Sometimes he gave talks, or lectures, to explain scientific discoveries. Often his lectures were for scientists or other adults. But he also gave talks to children, to help them understand science.

Spinning Turbines

A generator in a power plant converts mechanical energy, such as the spinning of a coil around a magnet, into electricity. But where does the mechanical energy come from—what makes the coil spin? The answer is a device called a **turbine**. This is a machine that can be turned by flowing liquid or gas.

A pinwheel is a type of turbine. If you hold a pinwheel up in the air on a windy day, the moving air pushes the blades of the pinwheel and causes them to spin. A power plant turbine also has blades. The blades are on one end of a long heavy pole, or rod. The other end of the rod is

In many power plants, steam turns the blades of a turbine, making a rod turn. The rod is connected to a generator. When it turns, then either a magnet or a coil turns in the generator, producing electricity.

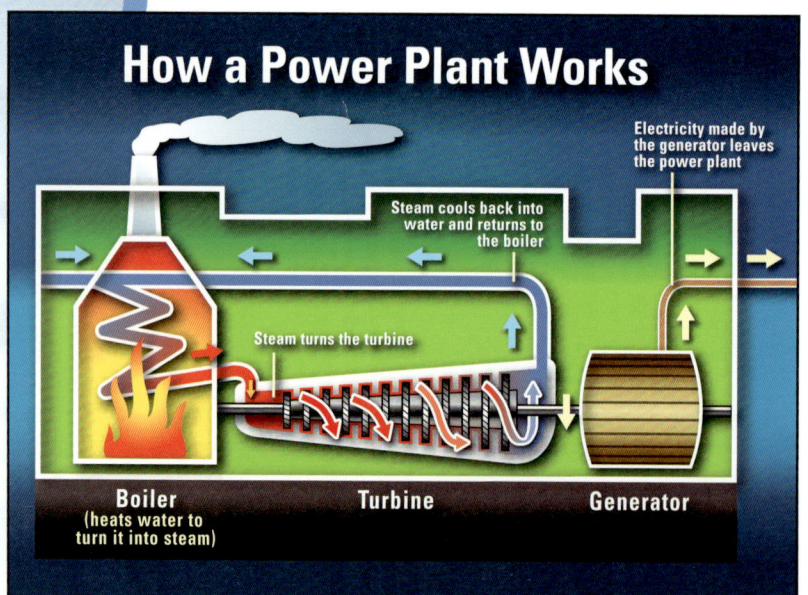

connected to a generator's coil or magnet. Often, falling water or moving steam pushes the blades of the turbine and makes them turn. This makes the rod they are attached to turn. And when the rod turns, then the coil or magnet in the generator turns too—and electricity is created.

Making Steam

In power plants that use steam to turn the blades of the turbine, where does the steam come from? Many power plants burn some type of fuel to heat water and turn it into steam. Common types of fuel that are used are coal, oil, and natural gas. But this can cause problems.

When coal, oil, or gas is burned in a power plant, smoke gets into the air that can have harmful chemicals in it. Dirty, or polluted, air can harm people and other living things. It may also change Earth's climate. Many countries are trying to make more of their electricity in power plants that do not need to burn coal, oil, or gas.

DID YOU KNOW?

Huge Turbines

Some power plants have turbines that are more than 72 feet (22 meters) across (72 feet is about the length of five cars).

Moving Electricity

The huge amount of electricity made at a power plant is useful only if it can be sent to where it is needed. Electricity travels from the power plant to other places using a system of special equipment, thick power lines, and tall steel towers called pylons.

A power plant can generate many thousands of volts of electricity. There is plenty of push from this voltage to get the current to nearby areas. Many power plants, though, are not in towns or cities. The electricity has to travel many miles before it can be used in homes, schools, and businesses. More volts are needed to push the electricity over great distances.

High-voltage electricity often travels long distances from a power plant in power lines held up by tall steel pylons.

Changing the Voltage

When the electricity leaves the power plant, it first goes through a special type of equipment called a step-up transformer. A transformer is a device that increases or decreases voltage. A step-up transformer increases voltage, which allows the electricity to travel great distances.

Most homes, schools, and businesses cannot safely use electricity at very high voltages. When electricity from a power plant reaches a city, for example, it is sent through one or more substations to lower the voltage. A substation is often a small building that has transformers in it. These transformers do the opposite of the step-up transformers. They are called step-down transformers. Substation transformers change high voltages to lower voltages that can be used.

DID YOU KNOW?

The Smallest Transformers

Not all step-down transformers are big. Cell phones and laptop computers need very little voltage to run. The same is true for digital music players. The cords that come with these devices have built-in transformers that bring voltage down from 110 volts to about 6 volts. The transformer usually looks like a small black box (see photo above).

In the Home

You can't see it, but there are hundreds of feet of wire behind the walls of your home. This wire makes up the many circuits that carry to all parts of the home the electric current that has come from the power plant.

Different kinds of switches are important parts of circuits. Switches can create breaks in the circuit. You control some switches yourself. Every time you flip a light switch on or off, you are controlling the flow of electricity.

Special Switches

There are also special switches called **circuit breakers**. Usually,

Plugging in too many appliances to the same circuit can overload that circuit and cause the circuit breaker to switch off.

every circuit in the home has one. These switches automatically flip off and break the circuit if there is a power surge. In a power surge, too much current comes through the wires all at once. A surge may happen during a storm, if there is a great deal of lightning.

A power surge can cause problems. Too much current going through a circuit all at once can cause the wires to become very hot or even start to burn. It can also damage things like televisions, computers, and other electrical devices. But when the circuit breaker switches off, the flow of electricity stops, and problems are avoided. When whatever caused the circuit breaker to flip off is taken care of, an adult can flip the circuit breaker switch back to the ON position.

Many homes have a metal box like this one with a circuit breaker for each of the home's circuits.

DID YOU KNOW?

Overloading Circuits

All the electrical outlets in a particular room are often on one circuit. If too many electrical devices are plugged into the same circuit, they start pulling too much current through the wires. This is called overloading the circuit, and it can cause a power surge. To prevent danger, the circuit breaker will switch to the OFF position. Even though circuit breakers will usually prevent a safety hazard, it's a good idea to avoid putting too many devices on one circuit.

Sharing Electricity

It's a hot August day. Every air conditioner and fan in your neighborhood is running. Suddenly, the lights in your home flicker. The light bulbs dim. The television blinks off. On days like this, there is a huge need for electricity. Sometimes, the need is much greater than the amount of electricity the power company can be deliver. When this happens, there is a **brownout**.

A brownout occurs when a power company reduces the amount of electricity being delivered to homes and businesses. The company's power plants cannot produce enough electricity for everyone.

Networks such as the one shown here can help power companies many hundreds of miles apart to share electricity when needed.

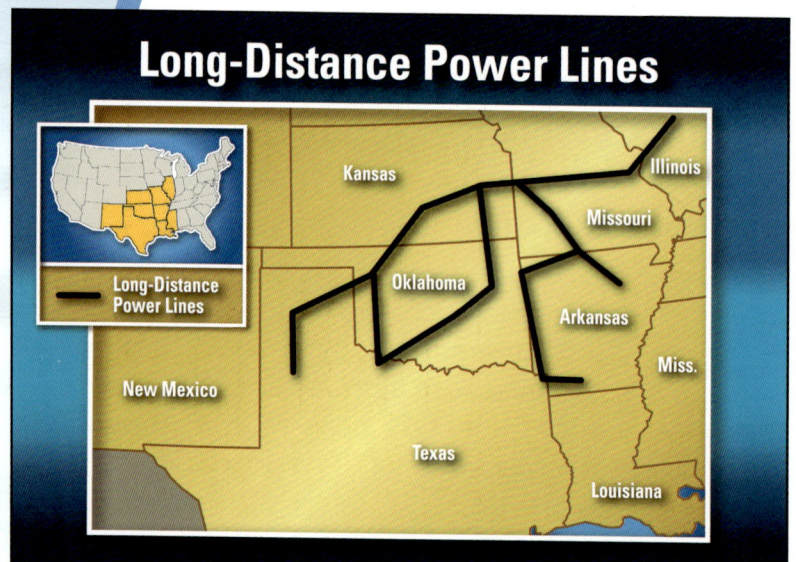

A **blackout** is the loss of all electric power. Sometimes a blackout occurs when a power plant stops producing electricity. Perhaps a piece of machinery at the plant stops working.

In most cases, though, blackouts are caused by something that prevents the delivery of electricity to homes and businesses. Bad weather is a common cause of blackouts. For example, storms can cause power lines to snap.

Forming Networks

Power companies try to avoid brownouts and blackouts by linking their power lines together to form a network. A network allows a power company in one area where a lot of electricity is needed to "borrow" some electricity from a plant far away. There are networks throughout the United States and Canada.

Downed power lines and ice-covered trees in Montreal, Quebec, in 1998.

DID YOU KNOW?

Help in a Storm

Power companies in New England sent electricity to Quebec, Canada, in 1998 to help out during a winter emergency. A very bad winter storm had caused many power lines in Quebec to become coated with ice. The ice weighed down the power lines so much that they snapped. Millions of people lost power.

Looking to the Future

A great deal of the world's electricity is made in power plants that burn coal, oil, or natural gas. Burning these fuels may harm the environment. Also, there is a limited supply of these **resources**. Once they are used, they are gone forever. Scientists are working on ways to make more electricity using other resources that won't run out.

Energy from the sun can be turned into electricity by **solar panels**. Areas with strong, steady winds can use that wind as a resource. Wind can turn windmills. Windmills can turn a turbine and a generator to create electricity.

Video game players run on electricity. Turning off electrical devices when they're not being used means that electricity won't be wasted.

Using Less

Using less electricity is another way to conserve resources. Many electrical devices today—air conditioners and refrigerators, for example—are made to use less electricity than the same kinds of devices used in the past. You may have seen energy efficiency tags on appliances in a store. Each tag tells you how much—or how little—electricity the device uses. Many people try to buy appliances that are the most energy efficient and use the least electricity.

You can also reduce the amount of electricity you use in your daily life. A small action such as turning off lights in a room when you leave it means less electricity is used. The same goes for turning off televisions or computers when you're not using them.

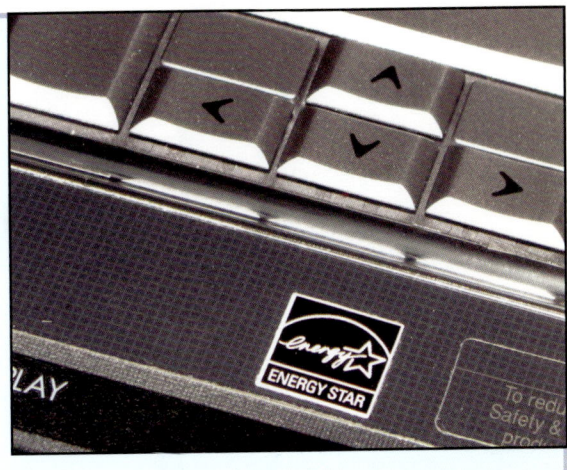

An Energy Star sticker on a device that runs on electricity means the device has met energy efficiency guidelines set by the U.S. government.

DID YOU KNOW?

How Much Electricity?

This list shows you how many watts of power some common electrical devices use when they're on:

clock radio:	4 watts
television:	55 to 90 watts
video game player:	70 to 165 watts
window air conditioner:	500 watts

Glossary

alternating current—**Current** that changes direction back and forth as it flows through a **circuit**.

ampere—A unit of measurement for the number of **electrons** flowing past a point in a **circuit** in one second. Often called amp for short.

atoms—Tiny particles that make up all **matter**.

attracted—Pulled toward something.

blackout—A total loss of electric power.

brownout—A partial loss of electric power.

circuit—A closed path that electricity travels along.

circuit breaker—A **switch** that will automatically break a **circuit** if there is too much **current** flowing through it.

conductor—A material through which electricity can flow easily.

current—A stream of **electrons** moving continuously along a path.

direct current—**Current** that always flows in one direction.

electrons—Particles in an **atom** that carry a negative charge.

filament—The metal wire in a light bulb that heats up to give off light.

generator—A machine that changes the energy of motion into electricity.

insulator—A material through which electricity cannot flow easily.

matter—What all things are made of.

neutrons—Particles in an **atom** that do not carry any charge.

protons—Particles in an **atom** that carry a positive charge.

repel—To push something away.

resources—Things that can be used.

solar panels—Devices that convert energy from the sun into electricity.

switch—A device that completes or breaks a **circuit**.

turbine—A machine that turns to move a magnet within a coil or to move a coil around a magnet to create electricity.

voltage—The push that makes electric **current** flow along a path.

volt—A unit of measurement for the amount of push moving an electric **current**.

watt—A unit of measurement for the power of an electric **current**. It measures how many **amperes** are being pushed by how many **volts**.

To Learn More

Read these books:

Buller, Laura, and Steve Parker. *Electricity*. New York: Dorling Kindersley, 2005.

Cooper, Christopher. *Electricity: From Amps to Volts*. Chicago: Heinemann Library, 2004.

Searle, Bobbi. *Electricity and Magnetism*. Brookfield, Conn.: Millbrook Press, 2002.

Look up these Web sites:

electric circuits
http://www.thetech.org/exhibits/online/topics/12b.html

electric power plants
http://www.osha.gov/SLTC/etools/electric_power/illustrated_glossary

electricity
http://science.howstuffworks.com/electricity.htm

Key Internet search terms:

Electric circuits, electricity, energy, power plants

Index

Air pollution 28, 31
Alternating current 15
Amperes 14–16
Atoms 6–7
Attraction and repulsion 7

Batteries 13, 15, 16
Blackouts and brownouts 26, 27

Circuit breakers 24–25
Circuits and switches 12–13
Computers 15, 17, 29
Conductors (electricity) 10–11
Converters 17
Copper 10–11
Current (electricity) 10–11, 14–15

Delivery of electricity 22–23
Direct current 15
Discharge, electrical 8–9

Electrons 6, 7, 8, 9, 11, 14

Faraday, Michael 18, 19
Filament 11
Flashlights 13, 14
Franklin, Benjamin 7
Fuels 21, 28

Generator 18–21

Heat 11
Human body (as conductor of electricity) 11

Insulator 11

Light bulbs 10, 11, 17
Lightning 9

Magnets 18–19
Magnetic field 18–19
Making of electricity 18–21
Matter 6
Measuring electricity 14–17
Mechanical energy 18, 20

Neutrons 6
Nucleus (atom) 6

Power plants 19, 20–21
Power surge 25
Protons 6, 7
Pylons 22

Refrigerators 12, 15
Resources, conservation of 28–29

Sharing of electricity 26–27
Static electricity 8–9
Steam, source of (power plants) 21
Switches, functions of 12–13, 24–25

Transformers 23
Tungsten 11
Turbine 20–21

Uses of electricity 4–5

Voltage 16, 17, 19, 22, 23

Water (conductor of electricity) 11
Water power 20
Watts 17, 29

About the Author
Barbara J. Davis has written books on science topics for kids for more than fifteen years. She has published books on ecosystems and biomes, as well as on earth science subjects.

J 537 D

Davis, Barbara J.
Why Do the Lights Turn On?
12/10/09